STRATHNAVER

a visual exploration in the heart of Sutherland North Scotland

Erika Meershoek: artwork & poetry
Dennis Moet: photography & mapping

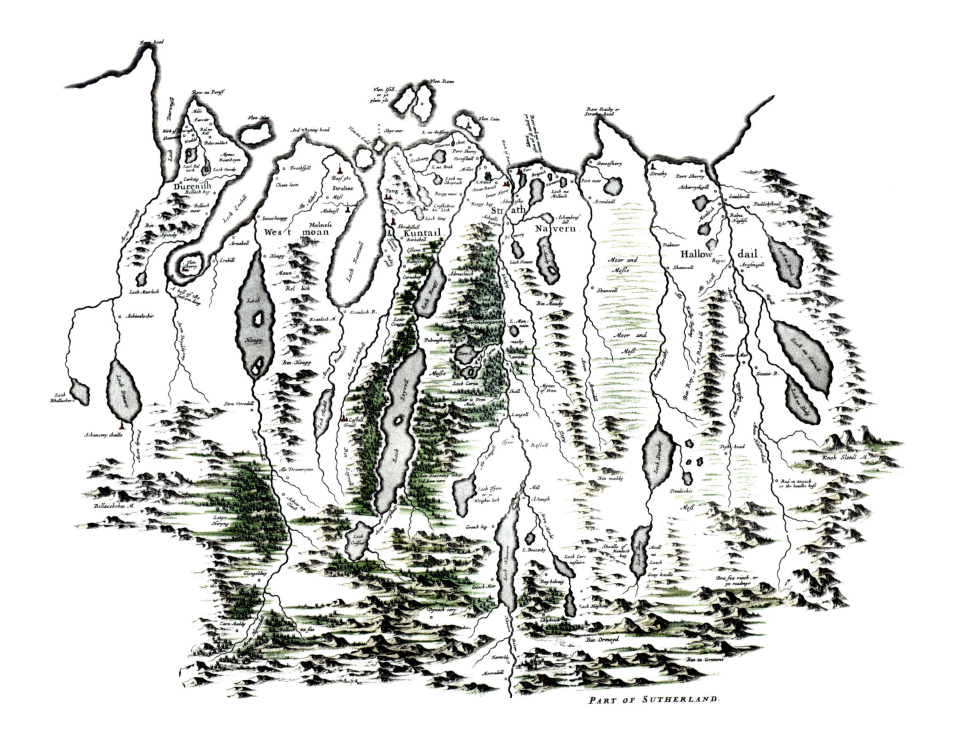

PART OF SUTHERLAND.

FOREWORD

'The stream invites us to follow', wrote WH Hudson in 1903, 'the impulse is so common that it might be set down as instinct; and certainly there is no more fascinating pastime than to keep company with a river from its source to the sea'. In 2008, Erika Meershoek and Dennis Moet accepted the invitation of the River Naver, and over the subsequent 18 months they kept it company from where its waters rise, on the north-west slopes of Ben Klibreck and the eastern corries of Ben Hope, down through burn and stream into long Loch Naver, then out into the River Naver itself and along its northerly course, past Bronze Age tumuli, Iron Age brochs and cleared nineteenth-century townships, past alder, ash, birch and pine, through ling, broom, gorse and azalea, over granite, feldspar and mica schist, in snow, sunshine, mist and dusk, always northering, northering…and finally out to where the river meets the Atlantic Ocean, where salt and fresh mingle, by the vast tawny dunes that mark the Naver's mouth.

What they understood, by the time they reached the river-mouth, by the time they had experienced the valley in high hot summer and in a winter so deep that the temperature fell to –22 degrees at Altnaharra, was that no single response would be adequate to the valley. That our word 'landscape' is really a futile group-noun for the uncountable and unsummarisable aspects of geology, meteorology, human geography, fauna, flora, the fall of light and the run of water, as well as the unrepeatable individual experience of moving through a place, that together make up what we easily call 'place'. And so they began to try out different forms of representation that might differently fit the land. Finding, mapping, keeping, collecting, writing, painting, photographing, casting, imagining, following, talking, drinking: these are some of the many verbs or acts that have gone into the making of this book, whose variety testifies to the versatility of Erika and Dennis as artists.

They have shown a readiness – a restlessness – born of their subject. Weave, wave, flux, strata: these are the actions that emerge as tropes, even obsessions here. Again and again, images return to siltings and to layerings, geological and hydrological, chromatic and human. Other works acknowledge the powerful reverberation that certain landscapes can set up between the radiantly specific and the mythical-allegorical. I think here of the pebbles of granite, nestling inside their metal leaves, whose multi-coloured surfaces are at once maps of entire tiny planets – and the insides of golfballs or sucked gobstoppers. I think too of the page of cloud pictures, with their rents and tears, their parahelia and storm-strata, at once the frame-by-frame account of a Gotterdammerung – and a child's stamp collection.

I began with Hudson; Erika and Dennis end with Seneca's witty one-liner on water: 'When you have come to understand the true origin of rivers, you will realize that you have no further questions.' There is, of course, no knowing the true origin of rivers, as there is never an end to further questions. The water of the Naver spills into the sea, where it forms rain-clouds and falls again as fresh, up on the high gneiss slopes of Ben Hope, and so the loop is closed, the circuit completed, the questions left unanswered. This lovely book pries at the mystery of place but is, in the end, content with not-knowing. Its final image acknowledges this: a wide-angle black and white still of the estuary, light falling from high overhead through a gulf in the clouds, the vertical fall of the photons perpendicular to the lateral roll of the waves, the river's mouth open, the photograph itself dense with beauty and absolutely devoid of certainty.

Robert Macfarlane, April 2010

ORIENTATION

The topology and identity of Scotland are inextricably linked to water. With a land area of about 79,000 sq km, Scotland has over 30,000 fresh water lochs and 6,600 river systems.

The Naver is the largest river of the county of Sutherland. Naver, in Gaelic Nabhair, is a pre-Celtic name meaning moist, cloud and mist. The catchment basin of the river is enclosed by Ben Hope and Ben Klibreck. The area itself rises about 200 m above sea level. The local annual rainfall average is 1200 mm. Loch Naver is the headwater of the River Naver which flows 31 km north to Torrisdale Bay. The principal tributaries are the River Vagastie, Mudale and the Mallart. The southernmost headspring is close to Crask Inn.

The characteristics of Strathnaver reflect periods of geology, glaciation, civilization and clearances. The first settlers arrived some 6000 years ago in the strath. For centuries, the valley was heavily populated with self-sufficient communities. People's way of life hardly changed from generation to generation, until the land-owners between 1814 and 1822 cleared the strath of the crofters to make way for Cheviot sheep. The inhabitants moved to the coast to establish themselves as crofter-fisherman. Many eventually emigrated overseas. With them the nymphs also departed.

Today Strathnaver is scattered with former settlements, some new private enterprises, anglers and a merciful stillness. The scenery of the Upper Naver, from Altnaharra to Syre, is typically Highland. From that point onwards the river is bordered by woodland and fertile meadows until it reaches the wide sands and wandering dunes at the Naver Mouth to the west of Bettyhill.

The stirring history and splendour of the riverine landscape remain there to be discovered by the wanderer.

ERICACEAE
Loiseleuria Desv.

Calluna Salisb.

summer 2008

C. vulgaris (L.) Hull (107, 108) Heather
On heaths, moors, woods and dunes. Common, widespread.

CREICH LAIRG ROGART DORNOCH GOLSPIE CLYNE LOTH KILDONAN
ASSYNT EDDRACHILLIS DURNESS TONGUE FARR

Erica L.

E. tetralix L. (107, 108) Cross-leaved Heath
Damp heaths, moors and woods. Common, widespread.

CREICH LAIRG ROGART DORNOCH GOLSPIE CLYNE LOTH KILDONAN
ASSYNT EDDRACHILLIS DURNESS TONGUE FARR

E. cinerea L. (107, 108) Bell Heather
Dry heaths and moors. Common, widespread.

CREICH LAIRG ROGART DORNOCH GOLSPIE CLYNE LOTH KILDONAN
ASSYNT EDDRACHILLIS DURNESS TONGUE FARR

LEGUMINOSAE
Ulex L.

spring 2009

U. europaeus L. (107, 108) Gorse
Roadsides, old woodlands, heaths. Common, widespread.

CREICH LAIRG ROGART DORNOCH GOLSPIE CLYNE LOTH KILDONAN
ASSYNT EDDRACHILLIS DURNESS TONGUE FARR

Sarothamnus Wimm.

S. scoparius (L.) Wimmer ex Koch (107, 108) Broom
Amongst scrub and on heaths. Common in the east, sparse (introduced)
in north and west.

CREICH LAIRG ROGART DORNOCH GOLSPIE CLYNE LOTH KILDONAN
ASSYNT —— DURNESS TONGUE FARR

Unlike the Tartan lines
layered in stiff pattern,
the water flows like silky
sheets in the wind.
Soft and elegant but
determined to go all the way.
Pebbles and cobbles
like islands in the stream,
making waves and twirls,
flirting around trout hiding places.
In and out of deep holes,
from the springs into the loch,
through the strath.
Ending with changing tides
into the sea.

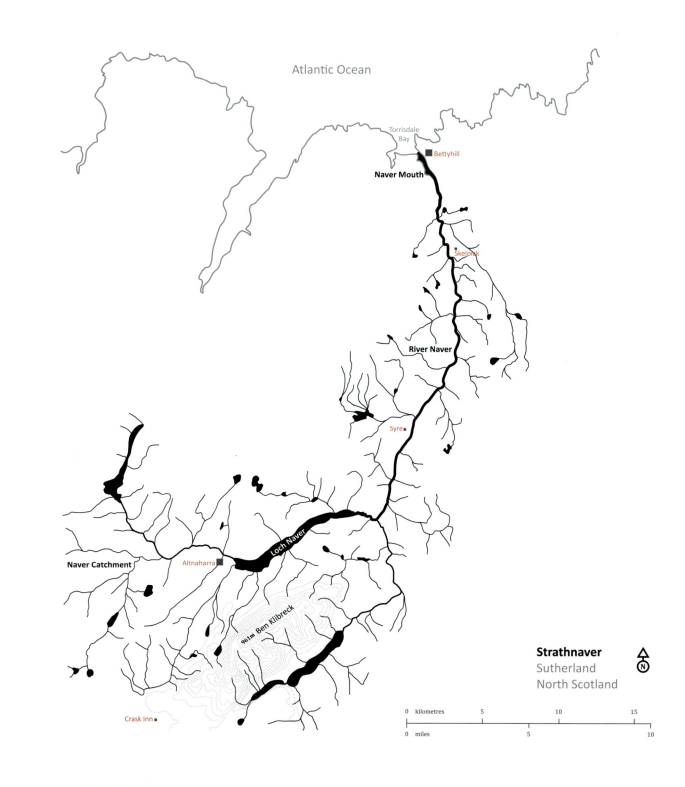

Atlantic Ocean

Torrisdale
Bay

■ Bettyhill

Naver Mouth

Skelpick

River Naver

Syre ■

Naver Catchment

Loch Naver

Altnaharra ■

961m Ben Klibreck

Crask Inn ■

Strathnaver
Sutherland
North Scotland

| 0 | kilometres | 5 | 10 | 15 |

| 0 | miles | 5 | 10 |

NAVER CATCHMENT

The white world is silent
all sound is muted
by the blanket of snow.

The loch has disappeared under
a huge flow formed windowpane
grooved by the wind.

Cottages are snoring from
the wood- and peat burning stove
working hard to keep the families at ease.

In this whimsical white winter
time comes to a hold while life goes on
in its remote homes.

Allt na h-Eirbhe Hamlet

Where the stream flows through the hamlet,
there it lays, apparently untouched by modernity.
Right there, at the shore of the loch,
where pearls once were gold
but were trade in for salmon and trout.
Where men tied their own flies
drunk a single malt, proud as a peacock
with their best catch of the day.
That's the place where fly fishermen gathered round
during decades of fiery gaming and play until thick
cold clouds fell in and silenced the rooms.
Years it took to open up the air but finally even the sun
got back in and reluctantly the fishermen returned;
Voices in the house from people bringing in Wellingtons
and waders and fisherman's yarns could be heard again
from the tartan sofas near the open fire place.
Looking over the loch (dear Ben in the back),
the brightness of the day is part of the moment
as a witness in time.

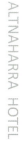

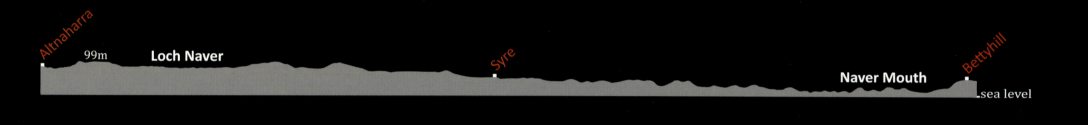

Altnaharra
99m Loch Naver
Syre
Naver Mouth Bettyhill
sea level

| 0 | kilometres | | 5 | | 10 | | 15 | |
| 0 | miles | | | 5 | | | | 10 |

contour Bettyhill Road (B873 - B871)

N

We do not see the "space" of the world; we live our field of vision.
We do not see the "colors" of the world; we live our chromatic space.

Maturana & Varela

From all over the world
messages wrapped in paper,
letters of love and confidence,
birth and death,
are flown in or brought by ship.

Then carried on land
and moved further on
over Sutherland peat.

Finding its destination through
'the post office face'
at the foot of Ben Klibreck.
Hoping to be received in right hands
waiting to be answered.

CLIMATE

The climate of Strathnaver shows a range of variability.

The high area between Crask Inn and Altnaharra is classified as cool, wet, exposed with rather severe winters.

Altnaharra on the shores of Loch Naver has a much better climate. This area is described as cool, wet, moderately exposed with moderate winters.

Along the shores of Loch Naver on the Bettyhill road, the climate improves rapidly so that even at Syre, some 15 miles from the coast, the climate is classified as fairly warm, rather wet, moderately exposed with moderate winters.

Here I am

in the middle of the circle; the broch

looking out over the river.

I'm searching for something to recognize,

but all I can see is the past.

People and no sheep.

Men and women living a harsh life to survive.

The stone-circle, remains of the Sutherland history,

makes me embrace the beautiful landscape of today

while, at the same time,

I cherish the past in my heart.

LOCH NAVER

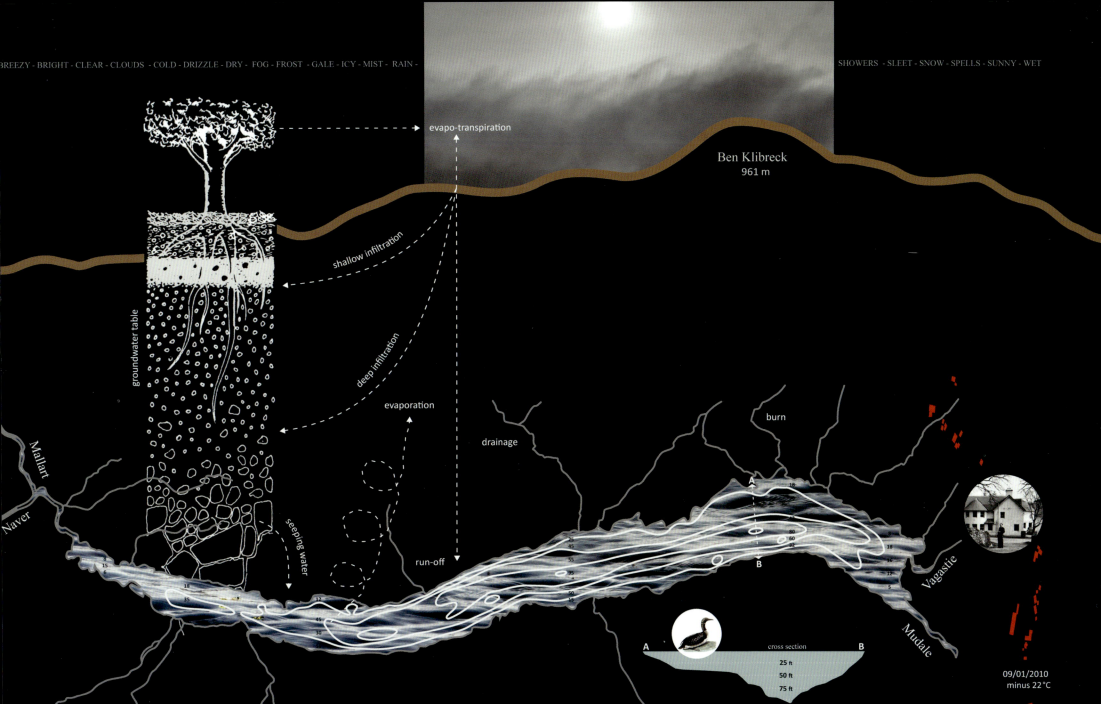

evapo-transpiration

Ben Klibreck
961 m

shallow infiltration

groundwater table

deep infiltration

evaporation

burn

drainage

Mallart

Naver

seeping water

run-off

Vagastie

Mudale

A

B

A   cross section   B

25 ft

50 ft

75 ft

09/01/2010
minus 22°C

Like the chalky layered oyster profile,
velvety soft,
the stream of purple and grey blue water
disappears in a rush while, at the same time,
wind on the water makes a mess of the stream.
All lines, bows and dots
around cobbles and pebbles;
joyful playground for salmon and trout.

DATE	WHERE CAUGHT	RIVER LAKE & RESERVOIR	BROWN TROUT	RAINBOW TROUT	SEA TROUT	SALMON	GRILSE	GRAYLING		
09										
23/2	Naver	J. Renne.				7 lbs				
24/2	Naver	J. Renna				1				
25/03	Naver	E. SSARKE				1				
24/03	''	S. JAJKOJSKI				1				
'' ''	''	S ''				1				
12/4	Buide	MEECH	3							
15/4	Loch Skerray	MEECH	4							
16/4	'' ''	MEECH	3							
23/4/09	NAVER	GAVIN HEPBURN				1				
25/4/09	''	SPENCER PATRICK				1				
2/05	BURGIE	S SMITH				1				

INDIVIDUAL WEIGHT		TOTAL WEIGHT		WEATHER	REMARKS
S/GS	OZS/GS	LBS/KGS	OZS/GS		
bs				Drizzle	Fresh but no sea lice
±lbs				"	Fresh but no sea lice.
				Horrific	LICED, SKERPIC FLATS.
				Windy	LICED, DAL HALLIARY
6				"	LICED DAL MALLART
¼				Windy.	amazing weather for time
±lb				fine/sunny.	of year !!
1lb				Windy.	
16				Fine, clear	Long tailed sea lice. Rock pool.
½ lb				Overcast & cool	Syre Pool — on stripped Collie dog.
18				Windy	LICED. COLLIE DOG. Rocky.

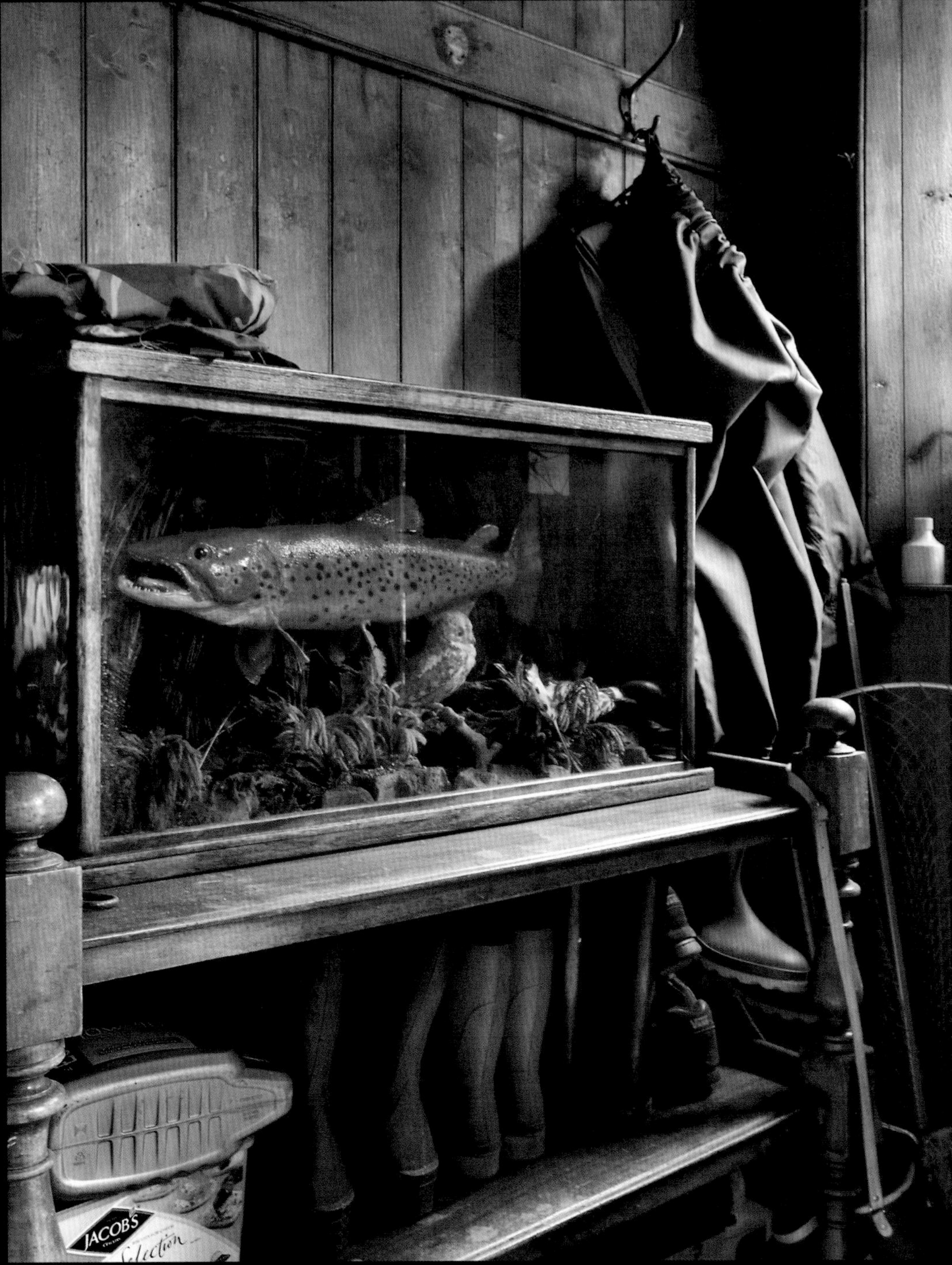
JACOB'S
Selection

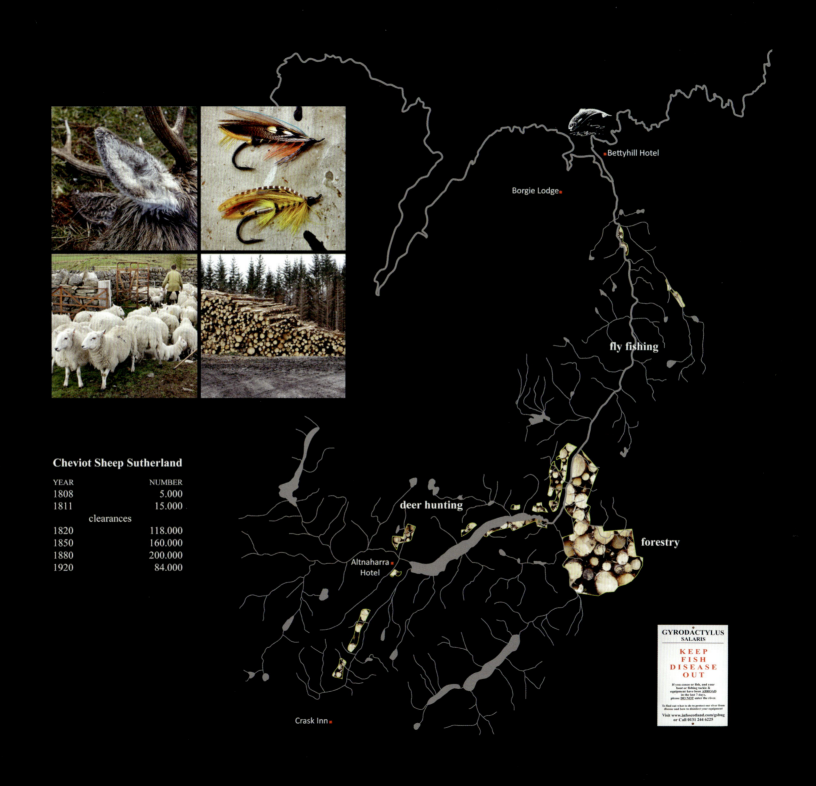

Bettyhill Hotel

Borgie Lodge

fly fishing

Cheviot Sheep Sutherland

YEAR	NUMBER
1808	5.000
1811	15.000
clearances	
1820	118.000
1850	160.000
1880	200.000
1920	84.000

deer hunting

forestry

Altnaharra
Hotel

Crask Inn

RIVER NAVER

Hymn for Tony

The red-roofed house of faith,

sober in its existence,

stands as a beacon in the bare, yellow landscape.

The people work hard; with the sheep,

with farming or with travellers.

No time for the word of god

or even for the song of joy.

It doesn't matter to the folks

because He is always near you,

in front of you or beside you.

Like your neighbors in the gorse- and broomfield,

they're there for you when you need them.

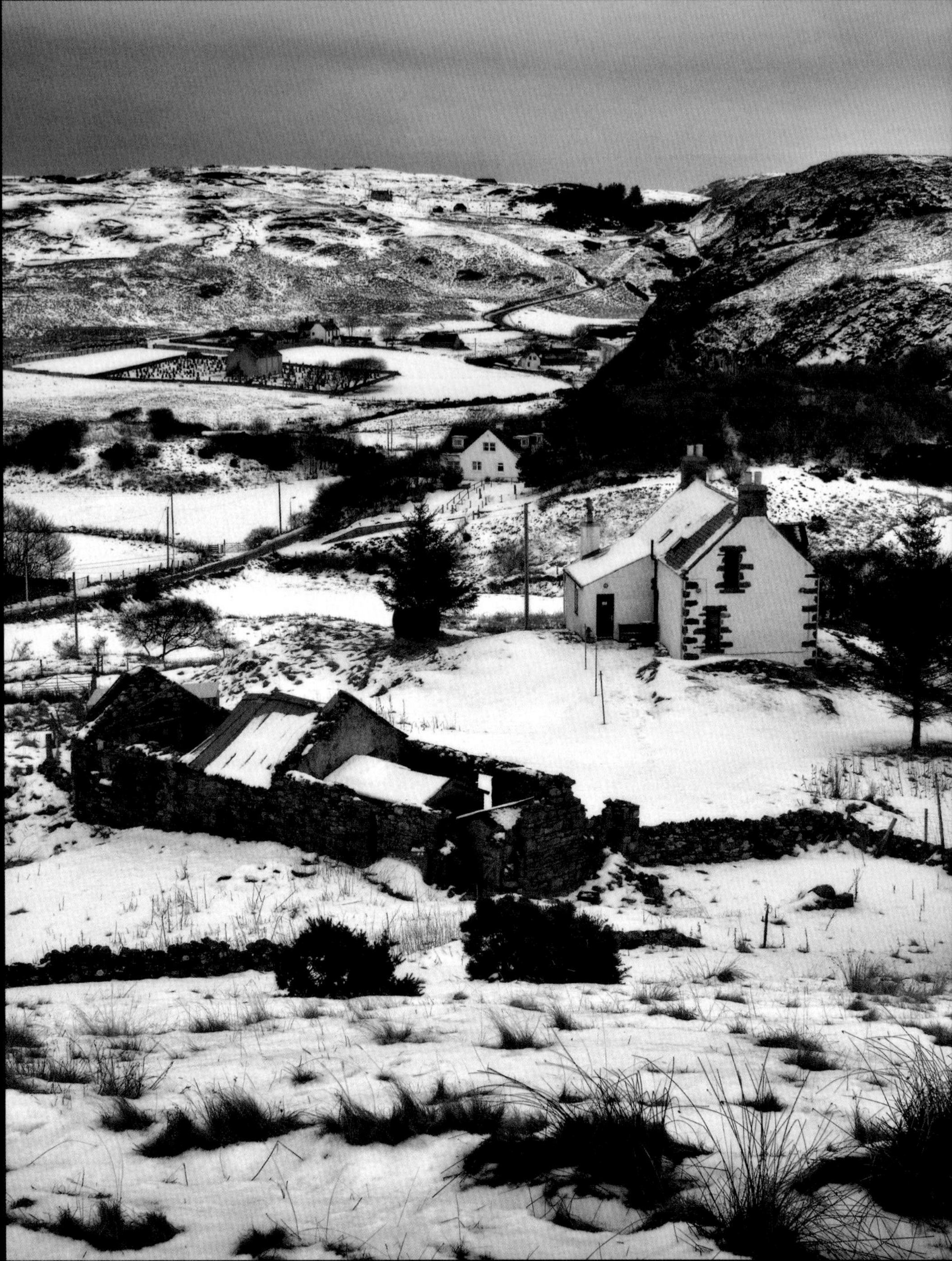

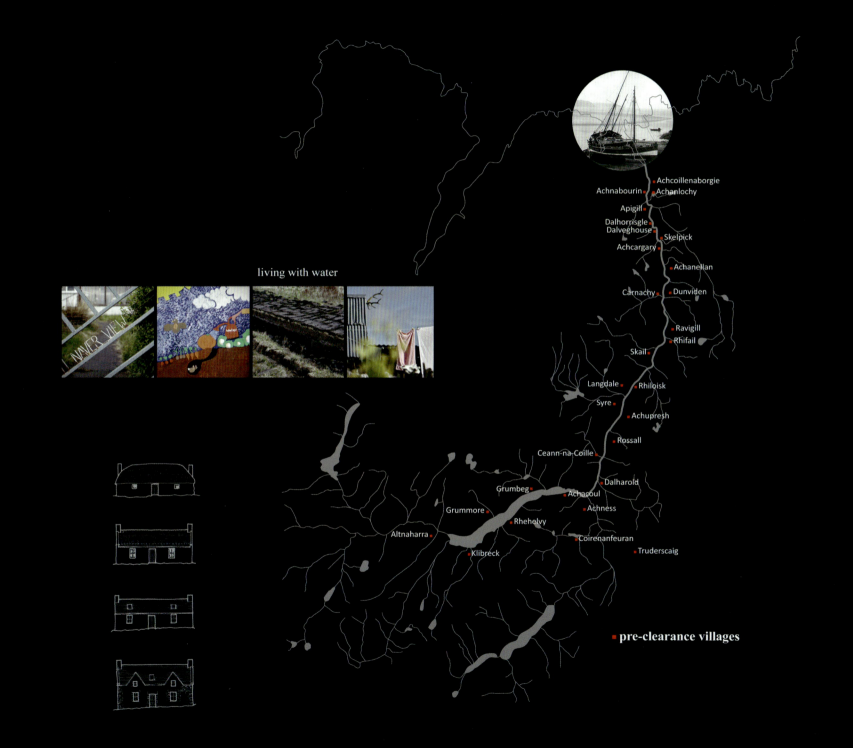

living with water

Achcoillenaborgie
Achnabourin
Achanlochy
Apigill
Dalhorrisgle
Dalveghouse
Skelpick
Achcargary
Achanellan
Carnachy
Dunviden
Ravigill
Rhifail
Skail
Langdale
Rhiloisk
Syre
Achupresh
Rossall
Ceann-na-Coille
Dalharold
Grumbeg
Achacoul
Grummore
Achness
Rhehelvy
Coirenanfeuran
Altnaharra
Klibreck
Truderscaig

■ pre-clearance villages

NAVER MOUTH

When you have come to understand
the true origin of rivers, you will realize
that you have no further questions

Seneca

AFTERWORD

This book is the result of our personal exploration of the essence of the unique, quiescent place Strathnaver. A remote valley in the heart of Sutherland marked by the constant flux of the elements and the slow pace of living orientated on the water. The Naver water course is like a vessel that runs through the strath, a vein of life and binding force.

'The wild places', written by Robert MacFarlane, directed us to Strathnaver and gave us some first insights of its splendour and raw history. It became our first source of inspiration. The first time we went there was August 2008; we found ourselves a purple world. May 2009 was the second time we went to the river valley; yellow was the colour of the day. The sense of place went beyond all…Our third visit was in January 2010, a muted white world of snow, still fascinating, still stunning and different every day.

It's always difficult to show what exactly it is that makes a place special. We tried to pay attention to the visual components of the cultural history as well as the underutilization, as nature in its pureness. What we did was a visual exploration of the different layers of the sense of place. We tried to catch the different spheres by which you can feel the quest for and exploration of the unique character of Strathnaver. The bleakness of the area makes us humble at first but the beauty is so stunning that you feel at one with the elements soon. Then you discover how the landscape, nature and culture are interwoven and influence each other. The balance between a livable landscape and a wild sublime place is delicate. To live your life in Strathnaver can be hard. Therefore it can't be otherwise that the earlier mentioned individual character of the landscape holds for the people as well… Rivers in particular enter deeply into our minds and lives, making our observations of them impossible to fully rationalize.

The photos were made with a digital- and a panoramic camera, the paintings with acrylic on canvas. The bronzes were made with field-material like heather twigs and sheep droppings.
The photos are realistic; the paintings are a 'site specific impression'; the bronze sculptures are a metaphor…To show the transformation force of Strathnaver, what happened and/or still is going on, therefore the mappings were created.

We want to thank everyone who helped us gathering information, telling us stories and showing us interesting spots; thanks for the great hospitality and for commenting on and correcting this book.

Erika Meershoek & Dennis Moet

COLOPHON

This edition of STRATHNAVER is limited to 300 copies.
Published by GIDZ-books
www.gidz.net

Printed by Ecodrukkers BV, Nieuwkoop the Netherlands
www.ecodrukkers.nl

ISBN 9781616277604

Available in the United Kingdom through Kevin Crowe, Loch Croispol Bookshop
Balnakeil Craft Village, Durness Sutherland IV27 4PT , Telephone (44)-01971-511777
lochcroispol@btopenworld.com
www.scottish-books.net / www.worldbookmarket.com

MIX
Paper from
responsible sources
FSC® C006253

Published with the support of:
Renate, Wendy, Martijn, Inge, Hedwig, Kees, Jeroen, Paul, Frans, Nina, Hanjo, Ellen, Aale, Clemens, Evelien, Gerard, Riet, Ludo, Tom, Ruud, Ard, Martin, Nelleke, Hans, Fred, Mariet, Harm Albert, Ann, Leo, Marijke, Bruno, Monique, Eric, Jacques, Jan, Marinus, Noud, Hanneke, Michiel, Leen, Lies, Gerrie, Lieneke, Bert, Jeltje, Remco, Henk, Arnold, Bea, Ad, Henny, Colin, Martin, Gaby, Irene, Rop, Rickerd, Trudy and Arend.

Special thanks to Kai and Mike Geldard, Ann and Bob Mackay, Jim Anderson and Robert Macfarlane.

COLLAGE

Ykema

Tuin- en Landschaps-
architectuur

books 11 / 2010

www.gidz.net